DEATH IN ENGLAND

Another Inspector Mirabelle Adventure (As well as his favorite)

by Sam Bobrick

SAMUEL FRENCH, INC.
45 West 25th Street NEW YORK 10010
7623 Sunset Boulevard HOLLYWOOD 90046
LONDON TORONTO

ISBN 0 573 69373 0 Printed in U.S.A.

IMPORTANT BILLING AND CREDIT REQUIREMENTS

All producers of *DEATH IN ENGLAND must* give credit to the Author of the Play in all programs distributed in connection with performances of the Play and in all instances in which the title of the Play appears for purposes of advertising, publicizing or otherwise exploiting the Play and/or a production. The name of the Author *must* also appear on a separate line, on which no other name appears, immediately following the title, and *must* appear in size of type not less than fifty percent the size of the title type.

CHARACTERS

DEATH
MICHAEL HEDGES
JANE THE MAID
IRENE HEDGES
INSPECTOR MIRABELLE
MISS CONSTANCE LAWSON
ALFIE CROWN
JONATHAN PIKE

Two Acts

One Set

#1 Pre-show music

Death in England

ACT I

Scene 1

TIME: An August afternoon.
PLACE: The entire play takes place in the study of the Hedges' London home.. The room is tastefully furnished with traditional antiques, as well as a spinet piano, a liquor cart, several chairs, a sofa and French doors that open to the garden.

MICHAEL HEDGES, an attractive looking man in his early fifties, sits in a wing back chair reading the London Times. *A somewhat younger MAN in a black hooded cloak stands waiting patiently at the other end of the room. His name is DEATH. Several moments go by.*

DEATH. You're frightened of me, aren't you?

MICHAEL. Yes. A bit. I believe so. Yes. You're right. I am.

DEATH. I know. Most people are.

MICHAEL. I imagine it's only natural.

DEATH. Yes. Very natural. Very.

(MICHAEL continues reading the paper.)

DEATH. Will you be much longer?

MICHAEL. Oh, no. Not much longer. So nice of you to allow me a last look at the *Times.*

DEATH. Well, it was a small request, and you're dealing with this so civilly.

MICHAEL. I am, aren't I?

DEATH. Yes. Most of the others I've come for tend to be very difficult in their final moments. They curse, they run about ranting, they throw things at me. But you seem to be taking your ... uh, exit so decently.

MICHAEL. (*Lowers paper.*) Well, I am British, you know.

DEATH. Yes. And it shows. It truly does.

MICHAEL. Thank you. (*Returns to the paper for a beat and then lowers it.*) Yet, I'm not really fond of the idea. It seems so unproductive. To be and then not to be.

DEATH. Yes. That is the statement, isn't it. Although some poor souls do find my coming for them a blessing. The sick, the weary ...

MICHAEL. And at times, I imagine, it's very necessary for the likes of Hitler and his ilk.

DEATH. Absolutely.

MICHAEL. God, the news is depressing tonight.

DEATH. Thank you.

(MICHAEL gives him a look.)

DEATH. (*Smiling.*) I'm not totally without humor, you know.

MICHAEL. (*Removes a cigarette from a nearby cigarette box.)* Mind if I have one last cigarette?

DEATH. If you must.

MICHAEL. I'd appreciate it. (*Offers him one.*) Care for one?

DEATH. Thank you, no. Never did pick up the habit.

MICHAEL. Good for you! (*Using nearby cigarette lighter HE lights up.*) By the way ... (*Indicates cigarette.*) ... is this what caused it?

DEATH. Most likely. Between tobacco and French food, it's amazing the human heart functions at all.

MICHAEL. So it's a heart attack then? (*Inhales cigarette.*)

DEATH. Yes.

MICHAEL. Painful?

DEATH. No, not very. Actually it's one of the more pleasant ways to depart. You won't know what hit you.

MICHAEL. Splendid. (*Takes another puff of his cigarette.*)

DEATH. By the way, is there any particular position in which you'd like to be found?

MICHAEL. I have a choice?

DEATH. Now and then I extend that courtesy.

MICHAEL. In that case, I guess right here in my favorite chair would be suitable.

DEATH. (*Disappointed.*) Oh, really.

MICHAEL. You sound disappointed.

DEATH. Your favorite chair. Frankly, it's a bit common.

MICHAEL. You'd rather I be more adventurous?

DEATH. Well, personally, I rather enjoy a racier end. For instance you could be found totally nude except for a pair of sneakers.

MICHAEL. A bit kinky, wouldn't you say?

DEATH. Yes, but extremely memorable. The press would make much more of it than an armchair departure. The very least you'd get is a page three in the tabloids.

MICHAEL. I prefer the chair.

DEATH. Oh, well, no harm in trying.

(JANE, a young maid, enters with a feather duster.)

JANE. Excuse me, Mr. Hedges. I won't be a minute. Is your guest staying for tea?

DEATH. What's that?

JANE. Are you staying for tea, sir? I shall be serving it on the half hour.

DEATH. You can see me?

JANE. Yes, sir, why? Are you supposed to be hiding?

DEATH. No. Not really. It's just that I haven't come for you and only those I come for are able to see me.

JANE. Well, I see you plain as day, and I love your robe. All wool, isn't it? I'll bet it set you back a pretty penny. By any chance, is there a little polo player on the left side?

DEATH. She can see me!

JANE. Of course.

MICHAEL. Something wrong?

DEATH. Yes, as-a-matter-of-fact, something is terribly wrong. She sees me, and I'm only seen by those I've come for.

MICHAEL. Well, she does see you. Don't you see him, Jane?

JANE. As plain as day, as big as life.

DEATH. Oh, my God, my God! Something is very, very wrong here.

MICHAEL. There is a God?

DEATH. Well, yes and no. It's an unusually complicated situation and really not my number one concern right now.

JANE. Excuse me, sir, but is this something I shouldn't be privy too?

MICHAEL. Jane, this gentleman is ... Death.

JANE. No!

DEATH. Yes.

JANE. Noooo! (*Walks around Death admiringly.*) You are Death?

DEATH. Yes, I am. And a bit addled at this point.

JANE. Death! Fancy that. Aren't you rather young for such an important position? I'll bet there must have been family connections somewhere down the line.

MICHAEL. (*Puts out cigarette in ashtray.*) You accept him as Death?

JANE. Well, lacking a formal education, I'm hardly qualified to get into a metaphysical discussion of what exists and what doesn't. On the other hand, it is a topsy-turvy world.

MICHAEL. Yes, that's true enough.

JANE. (*Folds up* London Times *and puts it away.*) Well then, Mr. Death. Will you be staying for tea or not?

DEATH. I ... I don't know. Let me think a moment. This is so ... so outrageous. The fact that you can see me. Unless, of course, I have come for you. How do you feel? Had the sniffles lately?

JANE. No. I'm sorry to say, I never felt better in my life.

DEATH. This is very, very upsetting. Look, do me a favor. As best you can, try not to see me.

JANE. I'll try, but I can't guarantee it.

(IRENE HEDGES, Michael's wife enters the room. SHE is an attractive woman in her late forties. SHE holds an invitation in her hand.)

IRENE. Oh, darling, we've just been invited up to the Ridgleys for the weekend. Isn't that marvelous? You'll be able to wear your new Safari jacket. Oh, excuse me. I didn't know you had company.

DEATH. Oh, no. She sees me too!

IRENE. I beg your pardon?

DEATH. (*Unnerved.*) You see me!

IRENE. Yes. Of course I see you. Why shouldn't I see you?

DEATH. Because I am Death.

IRENE. Death!

DEATH. Death!

IRENE. (*To Michael.*) Darling, I thought we agreed you would not bring your patients home anymore.

MICHAEL. I'm afraid he's not a patient, dear.

IRENE. Well, then it's obvious he should be. Death! Oh, this is a very sick, young man. Very sick.

DEATH. (*To Michael.*) You're a psychiatrist?

MICHAEL. Heavens no, a businessman. I operate a chain of sanitariums. Doing extremely well, by the way. I seem to have gotten into mental illness at the right time. I do have a group of psychiatrists working for me. A very odd bunch. Sometimes it's difficult to tell them from the patients. Lately, I stopped bothering.

IRENE. My husband does enjoy the company of some of his clientele, but after that awful experience with Mr.

Forsythe, I thought he had learned his lesson about bringing them home.

JANE. (*Shaking her head sympathetically.*) Poor Mr. Forsythe. To go through life thinking of himself as an aeroplane. He made these ghastly engine noises. I could hardly hear my vacuum.

IRENE. And then when hc threatened to take off from our third floor window ... It was nothing short of a miracle I was able to convince him he needed refueling.

MICHAEL. I swear, Irene, this chap is not a patient. He is Death, and I believe you are going to be spending this weekend in mourning.

IRENE. No!

DEATH. Yes. I am Death and I've come for your husband.

IRENE. Oh, no.

JANE. Life was so short, wasn't it, Mr. Hedges? I wonder if I should start making the sandwiches.

MICHAEL. For what?

JANE. For the condolence calls. The cucumbers are always the first to go.

IRENE. (*To Death.*) I don't know what your scheduling situation is like, your sovereignship, but could you possibly wait until after Sunday? Michael so loves visiting the Ridgleys. Their entire house is done in an African motif. Gives one the feeling of true adventure, not that what's going on here doesn't seem to fill the bill.

DEATH. No, I'm terribly sorry but I ... Michael? Wait a minute. Your first name is Michael?

MICHAEL. Yes.

DEATH. Not Lester? Lester Hedges?

MICHAEL. Goodness, no. Lester is my cousin. Lives several blocks down the street. I'm Michael Hedges.

DEATH. It seems I've made a dreadful error.

MICHAEL. Really? How marvelous. Not for Lester, of course, but for me. Oh, I feel so relieved.

DEATH. And I feel a bit chagrinned. I've never made a mistake like this before. I believe an apology is in order.

IRENE. I should think so! Imagine the damage a faux pas like this could cause. You could have frightened my poor husband to death. Of course, in that case, you would have been in the right house, wouldn't you?

JANE. Oh, Mr. Hedges. I am so happy for you. You have no idea how I hate peeling cucumbers.

DEATH. If you can, please, all of you, accept my sincerest apologies.

MICHAEL. To err is human.

DEATH. Yes, of course. That's what makes it so confusing. Oh, well, I'd better be getting around to Lester.

MICHAEL. It might be a good idea.

IRENE. Poor Lester. We so rarely see him these days, and now it seems even that's about to be minimized. I wonder if he's well?

JANE. I don't think I would bet on it.

MICHAEL. The future is fraught with unpredictables, isn't it?

IRENE. That's for certain. Well, now, Jane, would you please show Death to the door.

JANE. A pleasure. Right this way, sir.

DEATH. (*Uneasy and embarrassed.*) Well, uh, nice to have met you all and one day soon we'll do it again, I'm sure. Ta ta.

IRENE. Ta ta.

MICHAEL. And give Lester our best, not that it will mean anything now.

(The PHONE rings.)

JANE. Excuse me.

DEATH. Surely.

JANE. (*Picks up phone.*) Hedges residence. Yes, it is. Yes, he is. He did? He did? Pity. Yes, I'll tell Mr. Hedges immediately, although I think he rather expected it. Yes, good day. (*Hangs up.*) That was quick if I say so myself.

MICHAEL. Well?

JANE. It was your cousin Lester's landlord. I'm afraid he ... Cousin Lester ...

MICHAEL. (*Anxious.*) Yes?

JANE. He's dead.

IRENE. Poor, poor Lester. Never sick a day in his life, a fact which I'm sure we'll bemoan at the funeral.

DEATH. Nonsense! Utter nonsense! Take it from a very reliable source, he isn't dead.

JANE. No, sir. It's true. I heard it with my own ears. Mr. Hedges' cousin is no more.

DEATH. He can't be. I haven't gone for him yet.

JANE. And found in such a peculiar state. Totally nude except for sneakers. Fancy that.

DEATH. Impossible! It can't be, it simply can't be. I wasn't there yet.

MICHAEL. Well, he is dead and someone had to do it.

DEATH. Someone other than me? I don't like this at all.

(JANE screams.)

IRENE. Oh, dear, what was that for?

JANE. (*Loudly.*) Murder!

MICHAEL. Oh, come now.

JANE. It's true, sir. I've read enough Agatha Christie to spot it. (*Indicates Death.*) This gentleman here is Death, is he not?

IRENE. So he says.

DEATH. Of course, I am.

JANE. Well, then, if he didn't take your cousin Lester, someone else did.

MICHAEL. Yes? So? Go on.

JANE. (*Screaming.*) Murder!

MICHAEL. Will you stop that.

DEATH. She's absolutely right. Someone other than me has smote your cousin, Lester.

IRENE. But who? He didn't have an enemy in the world or so I would be expected to say. Who would have wanted to kill him?

JANE. (*Indicating Death.*) He would have.

DEATH. Yes, but that's different. That's my job. This is something else. Someone usurping my power. Someone tampering with me, with my omnipotence. Why? Why? And whom?

MICHAEL. (*Going to the phone.*) I don't know, but we shall soon find out.

IRENE. What are you going to do, dear?

MICHAEL. There is obviously some sort of treachery afoot and I fear we are in need of minds a bit more skilled at this sort of thing than ours. I'm calling the police.

DEATH. Yes, yes. By all means. Call the police. Please. (*Sits down dejected.*) I shall wait.

(MICHAEL begins dialing. ALL EYES are on Death. The stage DIMS slowly.)

End of Scene 1

ACT I

Scene 2

TIME: Later that afternoon. MICHAEL, IRENE and DEATH sit quietly in chairs as INSPECTOR EDWARD MIRABELLE paces the room. JANE is dusting.

INSPECTOR. Okay, now let's go over this once more. You say you are the victim's cousin.

MICHAEL. That is correct.

INSPECTOR. (*To Irene.*) And you are the wife of the cousin of the victim.

IRENE. Yes, but technically and by law a full cousin also.

INSPECTOR. Of course. (*To Jane.*) And you are the maid of the two cousins of the victim.

JANE. Yes, Inspector Mirabelle. I would have liked to have done more with my life but then I guess the world needs limited people too.

INSPECTOR. Yes, that's true. (*To Death.*) And you are Death?

DEATH. Yes. That's quite right.

INSPECTOR. Well, so far it all seems to check out. Still, I have this gut feeling that something is strange. Very strange.

DEATH. Then you suspect foul play?

INSPECTOR. A Police Inspector's job is to suspect everything and everyone.

JANE. Oh, my!

INSPECTOR. (*To Jane.*) Does that make you uneasy?

JANE. Yes, rather. Maids are blamed for everything.

MICHAEL. Frankly, Inspector Mirabelle, I'm surprised that you've accepted this situation at all. I've always thought of policemen as a very realistic bunch.

INSPECTOR. Yes. It makes one wonder about my judgement, doesn't it? Well, let me assure all of you that any negative appearance of my ability as a competent adversary of crime is a facade I carefully and cleverly use to disguise an acumen that even I, in all modesty, find astounding.

DEATH My, my. A public servant with a fine grasp of the English language. I applaud you, sir.

INSPECTOR. Thank you. Some of the fellows at the Academy chose ballet as an elective but I preferred grammar. Now then, the victim was found where?

MICHAEL. We already told you. In his flat two blocks down. 1120 Jamestown Place.

INSPECTOR. Then why may I ask was I called to this address?

IRENE. We thought it would be much more pleasant here, Inspector. Our cousin was a bachelor with extremely questionable taste. He quite foolishly tried to mix Oriental with High Tech. We all would have been very uncomfortable in those surroundings.

MICHAEL. In addition, Inspector, we have the necessary information. It seems the victim died of pneumonia.

JANE. With no clothes on and in a London flat, what would one expect?

INSPECTOR. Good point.

DEATH. But it shouldn't have been pneumonia. I had him down for a myocardial infarction.

INSPECTOR. A heart attack.

DEATH. A knowledge of the medical also. I am indeed impressed.

INSPECTOR. Yes. Before I joined the yard, I had thoughts of becoming a surgeon, among other things.

MICHAEL. Well, lucky for us....I mean that you've gone into crime ... detection.

INSPECTOR. Yes. *(To Death.)* Now then, you're quite certain the method of Lester Hedges death couldn't be an error on your part?

DEATH. Death never makes an error.

INSPECTOR. There is always a first time.

DEATH. With Death there is only a first time.

IRENE. I love your maxims, still my favorite is the one from Agamemnon. "Call no man happy till he is dead." I find it just brightens up the subject tremendously.

DEATH. The fact is, Inspector, in the eons of my tenure, I have never encountered a situation like this. It has me confused, thrown, a bit on edge. That's why I thought it best to seek professional help.

INSPECTOR. A wise decision. Now, the case, as I see it, is very clear cut. A death was performed by an unauthorized person.

JANE. How dastardly.

INSPECTOR. Yes, but who the culprit may be, is the mystery we must solve.

MICHAEL. How intriguing.

INSPECTOR. Of course. Now then, I have sent for a number of people I feel might help shed some light on this matter.

IRENE. How efficient.

INSPECTOR. Naturally.

(DOORBELL.)

INSPECTOR. That should be one of them right now.

DEATH. How convenient.

INSPECTOR. Isn't it.

JANE. I'll answer the door.

INSPECTOR. How sensible.

IRENE. I think we've gilded the lily.

(JANE leaves the room.)

MICHAEL. Do you really think you can solve this enigma, Inspector?

INSPECTOR. Enigmas are my life!

MICHAEL. Yes, but this is a bit on the supernatural side.

INSPECTOR. Which Scotland Yard finds curiously engrossing, since part of our training also includes two solid months of Ingmar Bergman films.

IRENE. I find it chock full of concealed significance. Death the strong, Death the final instrument, Death the most feared spectre in the universe up against the bloody wall. It is really something to think about, and we English do so love to think, don't we?

MICHAEL. Ponder, dear. I think the better word is ponder. We English ponder. The Aussies and the Yanks think.

IRENE. Of course. I stand corrected.

(JANE enters with a flamboyantly dressed young woman, MISS CONSTANCE LAWSON.)

JANE. Presenting Miss Constance Lawson, the victim's ahhhh ... lady acquaintance.

CONSTANCE. You're too kind.

JANE. I know.

INSPECTOR. I'll do the introductions, Miss Lawson. I am Inspector Edward Mirabelle of the Yard. This is Mr. and Mrs Hedges, the victim's cousins, their maid, Jane, and last but not least, His Unholy Eminence, Death.

CONSTANCE. Death, is he? Quite a good looker to have such a dark reputation.

DEATH. Death has many faces.

CONSTANCE. Really Well, when you come for me, wear that one. (*SHE winks and nudges Death.*)

INSPECTOR. Now then, Miss Lawson, we were trying to get to the bottom of who it is that was responsible for the untimely departure of one, Lester Hedges.

CONSTANCE. (*Pointing at Death.*) It wasn't him?

DEATH. No, it wasn't me. I assure you.

CONSTANCE. Well, then, I'm afraid it must have been me.

JANE. *(Screaming.)* Murder!

(THEY all look at Jane for a beat. SHE becomes very self conscious.)

JANE. Sorry.

INSPECTOR. You think you were the cause of Lester Hedges final breath, Miss Lawson?

CONSTANCE. It stands to reason. Mind you, there was no intended malevolence. It was just one of those things that happens occasionally in affairs of the heart.

IRENE. Can you clarify that, please?

CONSTANCE. I broke it. I broke his heart and he died.

MICHAEL. He died of pneumonia.

CONSTANCE. It is well known that a broken heart leaves men in so weakened a condition that they are open to all sorts of catastrophic suggestions. I'm sure Lester's end came when I told him I could no longer see him on his terms.

INSPECTOR. And what exactly were those terms?

CONSTANCE. Thursdays, between two and four at twenty-five pounds a visit.

INSPECTOR. And your terms?

CONSTANCE. Marriage, a home, a family.

INSPECTOR. And his counter terms?

CONSTANCE He said there was no way he would wed a slut.

INSPECTOR. And your counter-counter terms?

CONSTANCE. "Then piss off, Lester," I said. "I can no longer continue a paying relationship that is going nowhere." I left slamming the door furiously. To hell with that little creep, I thought.

IRENE. Good for you, Miss Lawson. I always felt Lester's existence went much too smoothly for his own good.

DEATH. An existence with no ups and downs is no existence at all.

JANE. That sounds so meaningful. Was it said by anyone famous?

DEATH. He might have been had I given him another two years.

MICHAEL. Wait, I don't understand. How could such a gross but basically minor falling out as the one Miss Lawson described, be responsible for Lester's fatal end?

CONSTANCE Very simply. As I closed the door behind me, I began to hear mournful sobs. I knew they had to be over our broken relationship. In my mind, I could all but see Lester's delicate aorta tearing to shreds, his face turning blue as the sea.

INSPECTOR. Mournful sobs?

CONSTANCE. Yes. Mournful. Painful. Definite sobs of woe. I guess in the final look-see of things, the lad really had it bad for me.

JANE. Oh, I'm so happy to hear that, Miss Lawson. It absolutely restores my faith in love.

CONSTANCE. And in some ways, albeit sad, mine too.

INSPECTOR. At the risk of shattering dreams, Miss Lawson, may I point out a very interesting fact, that being, that sobs of woe and the repression of the giggles sound one and the same.

CONSTANCE. No! They do? They don't! They do?

INSPECTOR. I'm afraid I have been around the pumpkin patch on that one too many times before.

CONSTANCE. Oh, my. The selfish little weasel may have been laughing at me.

INSPECTOR. It is very possible and most probable.

CONSTANCE. Fancy that. He giggled himself to death, and at my expense too. Well, in that case, I'm glad he's dead. Very glad indeed. (*SHE sits down sobbing.*)

IRENE. As a fellow woman, I must admit my sympathies are with Miss Lawson.

DEATH. My, what a bloody bastard this Lester was, although heaven knows the pains I've taken not to be judgmental.

INSPECTOR. Really? Not judgmental in the least?

DEATH. Absolutely not. Otherwise why then would I take Keats at age twenty-six and let Browning go to an over-ripe seventy-seven?

MICHAEL. (*Putting his hand on Constance's shoulder.*) Now, now, my dear. Don't feel bad. Lester was our cousin, but both my wife and I always felt, not quite a proper gentleman.

CONSTANCE. No. No, he was a gentleman with me. That's why I wanted to marry him. During the two hours I spent with him every week, he treated me like a queen.

INSPECTOR. How so?

CONSTANCE. He had me wear a royal red robe and call him Phillip. No one ever treated me like a queen before and I suspect, and rather fear, no one will long after poor, sweet Lester has rotted away in the grave he so richly deserves.

DEATH. Inspector, if I might interject ...

INSPECTOR. Of course. Feel free.

DEATH. Please bear in mind that how the victim died has nothing to do with this case. Whether he died naturally or unnaturally can be dealt with afterwards in your human halls of justice. The fact that he did die at all is what I want investigated. The fact that he did die without my infinite hand in it is what makes me the victim and everything else superfluous.

CONSTANCE. You care nothing about poor Lester?

DEATH. Lester was mortal. Mortal's die. True, a sad but nevertheless common occurrence. The problem here is that a foul deed has been perpetrated against my supreme position by forces unknown. That and that alone is the issue.

CONSTANCE. You are a cold Johnny, aren't you?

DEATH. In the grand scheme of things, Miss Lawson, I pride myself on simplicity. While my purpose is a powerful one, it is also quite to the point. So I say let's get on with it and not cloud the issue. Frankly, I am extremely disappointed at our rate of progress.

INSPECTOR. In my world, your Grace, it is sometimes necessary to take two steps backward in order to take one step forward.

MICHAEL. Inspector, I think it's two steps forward and one step back.

INSPECTOR. Is it?

MICHAEL. Yes. With your analogy we'd all be in the sea very shortly, wouldn't we?

INSPECTOR. You're right. I hope the botching of an old saw won't lead to a loss of confidence in my ability.

IRENE. Not at all, Inspector Mirabelle. In this day and age, what one says and what one means are quite often of a diverse nature anyway. Actually, it has become a necessary ability if one is to pursue a flourishing political career.

MICHAEL. Have you given any thought to entering the political arena, Inspector?

INSPECTOR. No, not really. I find crime much less treacherous as well as more sensible.

CONSTANCE. That's absolutely charming, Inspector.

INSPECTOR. Thank you. I must confess in all honesty, I've used it before.

DEATH. We are continuing to waste time.

INSPECTOR. Please forgive my small talk your Grace, but one of the first lessons we learned at the Yard is to never underestimate the importance of social repartee.

(The DOORBELL rings.)

JANE. Excuse me.

INSPECTOR. Certainly.

(JANE exits.)

INSPECTOR. Miss Lawson.

CONSTANCE. Yes?

INSPECTOR. By chance, did you notice anyone lurking about the premises of the late Lester Hedges?

CONSTANCE. Lurking about? It was early afternoon. No one lurks in the early afternoon. They mostly slink. Lurking is for evening. Slinking—afternoons. Sneaking for late at night, and in the morning, when one is fresh, a careful loiter.

INSPECTOR. An excellent rule of thumb. I must remember that ... Well, then, did you notice anyone slinking about?

CONSTANCE. No, no, I can't say that I did ... not anyone out of the ordinary ... except ...

INSPECTOR. Yes?

CONSTANCE. Except, perhaps for the bald midget who was sitting in a tree, but then sitting in a tree isn't really slinking about, is it?

INSPECTOR. A midget. That's odd.

DEATH. Really?

INSPECTOR. I've found that in every one of my cases where a midget was sighted, he represented a foreboding of evil.

(JANE enters with ALFIE CROWN, a man in his mid-forties.)

JANE. Presenting Mr. Alfie Crown, the victim's landlord.

DEATH. Look, allow me to reiterate this one final time. I am the victim. I would like courtesy where courtesy is due.

JANE. Well, aren't we on our high horse today?

ALFIE. Who's Inspector Mirabelle?

INSPECTOR. I am. This is Mr. and Mrs. Hedges, their maid Jane, Miss Constance Lawson ...

CONSTANCE. 'Lo, Alfie. Will I be seeing you this Monday?

ALFIE. I'm not sure. I may be behind bars.

INSPECTOR. And this is Death.

ALFIE. Pleased to make your acquaintances and then perhaps not.

INSPECTOR. Now what's this about the possibility of your being behind bars ?

ALFIE. I did it. I admit it. I killed him. I put an end to his life as sure as I 'm standing before you.

JANE. (*Screams.*) Murder!

INSPECTOR. Control yourself, my good woman.

JANE. Sorry.

ALFIE. It all started so innocently. "Good morning!," I says to him. "Good Morning!," he says back to me. "Bit nippy out don't you think?," I says to him. "Yes, it is," he says back to me. "I'll bet you'd be a bit warmer if you had on more than tennis sneakers.," I says to him. "Mind your own business, Auntie," he says back to me. "Drop dead," I then says back to him.

INSPECTOR. And?

ALFIE. And that's it. He did drop dead, didn't he? It was a curse. I cursed the bloke, I did.

JANE. (*Screaming.*) A curse!

(THEY all look at Jane for a beat.)

JANE. No more. I promise.

INSPECTOR. In this day and age, Mr. Crown, you can't really believe that curses work?

ALFIE. Normally, I don't. But there is that moment in life, that little eerie moment, when a door to the macabre opens just a speck and anything is possible.

INSPECTOR. No. No, I find it too hard to accept.

MICHAEL. Yet, Inspector, you accept Death. Wouldn't you say that was on the edge of the unholy?

INSPECTOR. But we are not dealing with death. We are dealing with one human being and another. We are dealing with your cousin, Mr. Lester Hedges and his landlord, Mr. Alfie Crown. If it were Death that cursed your cousin, that would be one thing. But it was just another ordinary person and that's where I draw the line. A human curse cannot kill anyone.

ALFIE. Well, mine did. I know it as sure as I'm standing right here in front of you. My curse did do the bloke in. May I drop dead if it isn't so. (*HE clutches his chest, gasps and falls to the ground.*)

IRENE. Oh, my.

INSPECTOR. (*Pointing menacingly at Jane.*) Whatever you do, you mad woman, don't you dare scream murder.

DEATH. (*Kneeling over Alfie.*) He's ... He's dead. Now there are two deaths that I had nothing to do with. Something dreadful is happening.

JANE. Maybe someone bought into the business.

MICHAEL. What do you make of it, Inspector? Has someone actually usurped Death's power?

INSPECTOR. It would seem that way, then again it might be that someone would like it to seem so.

DEATH. No, no, it can't be. I am Death and Death alone is Death.

INSPECTOR. In life there are no rules.

DEATH. We are talking about death.

INSPECTOR. It stands to reason that if there are no rules in life, there must be no rules in death since life and death are inexorably linked.

CONSTANCE. My goodness, you are a smooth talker, Inspector. I'm truly impressed. Are you free Thursday afternoons? I do think I would enjoy getting into your mind a little more.

DEATH. I am Death! I am Death and no one else can be Death as long as I'm alive ... in a manner of speaking.

MICHAEL. It really seems like you're in serious trouble, my friend.

DEATH. I am not your friend. I am no one's friend. And no one is mine. *(HE sits down and buries his head in his hands.)*

IRENE. You poor thing. May I have Jane get you a cup of tea?

DEATH. No thank you.

JANE. Maybe something to read? How about this morning's obituaries? That might cheer you up.

(DEATH gives her a look.)

JANE. Possibly not.

IRENE. If I may offer a suggestion.

INSPECTOR. Of course.

IRENE. This may very well be the solution to our dilemma. Why don't we just see if Death still has his old power?

CONSTANCE. You mean, see if he can still do away with someone? Strike a person dead? What a wonderful idea!

MICHAEL. Really now.

IRENE. Be practical, darling. I'm as opposed to haphazard extinction as the next person, but we've got to get on with this bizarre affair. Once and for all, we should see whether Death is who he says he is or actually just another everyday, Englishman who qualifies for one of your sanitariums.

MICHAEL. But what if he really is Death and can do what he says he can do? We would be responsible for taking an innocent person's life.

CONSTANCE. Yes, but then on the other hand it's been said that there are no innocent men in all of England, Ireland, and most of Wales.

IRENE. What do you think, Inspector Mirabelle?

INSPECTOR. A controversial suggestion, yet in it's own way, a possible step in the right direction.

JANE. Atta'boy, Inspector.

DEATH. (*Perking up.*) Well, even though I find this all a bit unethical, there is that nifty expression, any port in a storm.

(THEY all agree.)

DEATH. Now, who shall we elect for this rare opportunity? (*Points to Jane.*) How about her? Wouldn't it be nice not to hear that shrieking anymore?

JANE. (*Screaming.*) Mur...!

IRENE. (*Puts her hand over Jane's mouth.*) No, please, not Jane. She's been the backbone of this household for years. Besides, you have no idea what a chore it is getting new help to realize the importance of well polished silver.

JANE. Oh, Mrs Hedges, ma'am. I'll never forget your kindness, benevolent, yet completely impersonal. It's something quite special and shows great breeding.

IRENE. Thank you. It's so easy for one to carry concern a step too far.

INSPECTOR. The fatal mistake of most fallen societies. Now, it would seem to me that the most civilized approach to this proposal is to ask if there are any volunteers.

CONSTANCE. Oh, yes. Someone who will risk his life for the lot of us.

INSPECTOR. Exactly.

MICHAEL. Capital idea.

INSPECTOR. Thank you. Are there any volunteers?

(Silence.)

INSPECTOR. Hmmmm. Since World War Two that approach seems to be working less and less.

CONSTANCE. I think our best bet would be a stranger picked at random. Someone off the streets. That way there would be no hard feelings amongst us and maybe from time to time we'd still be able to see each other socially if some of us wanted.

JANE. A random death. How exciting. Almost sensual, I would say, if no one finds my being associated with that word a bit impudent.

DEATH. I've never taken anyone at random. I've always had a definite list. This may very well be a more stimulating approach.

INSPECTOR. Before we start, may I remind us all that we are not proceeding with this endeavor for any unsavory thrill, but merely to advance this case as quickly and humanely as possible and promptly clear up this taxing but beguiling quandary.

MICHAEL. In all good conscience, I find this approach totally questionable. I mean what if this person has a family, or is counted on for some matter of global importance. A random death can sometimes change the course of the entire world.

DEATH. I never considered the course of the world before. Why should I consider it now?

IRENE. Now there's a stumper for us if I ever heard one. How would you field this one, Inspector?

INSPECTOR. It's very possible this random removal may very well change the course of human events for the better, rather than for the worse. Actually, I've always felt that death should involve a smidgen of positive thinking.

CONSTANCE. My goodness, another splendid thought. The man's acumen knows no bounds.

INSPECTOR. It's really nothing that any defender of the law who graduated at the top of his class couldn't master.

DEATH. The top? I am extremely impressed.

INSPECTOR. Thank you. Frankly, those that know me assumed no less. Now then, what excuse shall we use to entice this unsuspecting and doomed chap into the house? Getting a total stranger to enter one's abode could be almost as tricky as keeping one out.

CONSTANCE. No one is comfortable walking the streets these days. We might as well be living in the States.

INSPECTOR. I propose that we put a sign in the front window announcing a room to let? We're almost certain to draw applicants with fewer attachments and thus eliminate a good portion of the guilt we're sure to feel at the funeral.

JANE. Oh, no. A lodger wouldn't do at all. I haven't gotten to the upstairs yet, and the spare room wouldn't show at its best. The last thing I would want to do is embarrass Mr. and Mrs. Hedges after they've been so remarkably decent to me.

IRENE. Frankly, if we must invite a total stranger into our house, I'd certainly prefer someone of a more refined nature.

JANE. Good for you, ma'am. I just pointed out to the plumber the other day what a woman of unusual taste you are.

CONSTANCE. Quality certainly shows, doesn't it? What is your suggestion, Mrs. Hedges?

IRENE. How about a sign that says "Antique Chest For Sale." I love antiques and I've always found it much easier conversing with unknown people I have something in common with.

INSPECTOR. Really? Quite frankly, I find talking about relics from the past yesterday's news.

CONSTANCE. I've got it. How about a sign that says, "Fortunes Told"? We could have a few laughs with the bloke before we inform him that Death is about to put the croaker on him.

IRENE. Oh, no. I couldn't bear a sign like that on our door. If it caught on, in no time at all this neighborhood would be infested with Gypsies and then, most assuredly, you can kiss the property values goodbye for a long time to come.

MICHAEL. What if we rang up the fire department? Certainly they'd send someone over if we said we smelled gas.

IRENE. Oh, but they'd send over a slew of people with a truck and all that and then they'd make such a mess banging in the door. What if we just reported a murder and sent for a policeman?

INSPECTOR. I *am* a policeman and that's exactly what you did.

CONSTANCE. Then I guess we're back to square one, aren't we?

DEATH. Now I see your plan. You people are obviously trying to drive me to suicide.

IRENE. Nonsense, although if you think about it, that would be cutting out the middle man, wouldn't it?

DEATH. Inspector, I want you to be aware that I am in a very fragile state.

(DOORBELL.)

MICHAEL. Now who can that be?

INSPECTOR. Whoever it is, let us all now agree that he be our choice for the uh ... journey.

ALL. Agreed!

INSPECTOR. Good.

(DOORBELL.)

JANE. Impatient sort. All the better. I'll get it. (*SHE exits.*)

IRENE. I hope what we're doing is right.

MICHAEL. Of course, it isn't. How can it be? We're sentencing a total innocent to his doom.

INSPECTOR. The values here are so muddled, aren't they? That's why I like this case best of all.

CONSTANCE. Let's hope none of us know our intended quarry. Death seems so much more palatable when it's not taken personally.

IRENE. You're so right. Like on the television news. It's getting so one can see any number of people dead or dying and not be that upset anymore. Of course, part of that could be attributed to sophistication.

DEATH. Listening to you people, it's very possible I may be experiencing my first headache.

(JANE ushers in a sinister looking MAN dressed in a loud, woolen tweed suit.)

JANE. Presenting Mr. Jonathan Pike.

INSPECTOR. Ahhh, Mr. Pike. I am Inspector Mirabelle. So nice of you to come by.

PIKE. Yes, I have come by, haven't I. It was most odd. I was actually on my way to who knows where, when I had a sudden urge to stop by and ask, if, by any chance, you have a room to let?

IRENE. Oh, my.

PIKE. Or an antique chest to sell?

IRENE. Oh, my.

PIKE. Or, if any of you good people might be able to tell my fortune?

IRENE. Oh, my, my, my, my, my.

PIKE. (*Offers calling card.*) My card.

MICHAEL. (*Taking card and reading.*) Jonathan Pike. Undertaker. Goodness, the symbolism is raging out of control today, isn't it?

PIKE. And, might I ask, in who's company I have the pleasure of being?

MICHAEL. Of course. I am Michael Hedges, successful businessman.

IRENE. And I am Irene Hedges. Successful businessman's wife.

JANE. (*Curtsies.*) Jane, devoted maid to the successful business man and his wife.

CONSTANCE. Constance Lawson. Lady of Mercy.

DEATH. Inspector Mirabelle, you have just met and my name is ... Death.

PIKE. Death? Is that a first or last name?

DEATH. An only.

PIKE. Interesting. So very nice to meet you all.

INSPECTOR. (*Indicating Alfie on floor.*) Oh, and that is the late Mr. Alfie Crown.

PIKE. (*To Alfie's body.*) And a belated how-do-you-do, although I think I know. (*Looks around.*) What a lovely home you have, Mrs. Hedges. Very expensively furnished. I must admit, I rather like being around quality more than not.

DEATH. Excuse me, but I don't think you were fully concentrating on the introductions. Sometimes, when one is introduced to several people, especially in a large group like this, a name or two is passed over without being given the proper significance.

PIKE. Yes, that does happen.

DEATH. Which is why I pointed this out. You see, when I introduced myself as Death, somehow I expected a larger response than merely ... "interesting."

PIKE. Really? Perhaps the reason is that I'm an undertaker. I am quite accustomed to death. Why should I be impressed by what is an every day occurrence in my line of work?

IRENE. Well, that satisfies me. How about every one else?

CONSTANCE. Suits me too.

JANE. Ditto.

MICHAEL. I believe we have a majority.

DEATH. What in blazes is wrong with you people? How can you all accept me so casually. I am Death! Death! A universal statement of fear, an axiom of the most chilling sort, an idea of monumental dread.

JANE. My goodness, am I the only one who is getting tired of this man blowing his own horn.

DEATH. (*To Pike.*) You do not stand in awe?

PIKE. In awe, no. In gratitude, perhaps, since your many appearances here and there have made me a financially secure man.

DEATH. You're missing the point.

PIKE. All the better then isn't it? In my line of work, one tries never to let emotions cloud the task at hand which at this point seems vague at best.

DEATH. (*Depressed.*) I've lost it! I've really lost it!

MICHAEL. Now, now. Just remember, it's always darkest right before the dawn.

DEATH. (*Reminiscing.*) Dawn! That used to be such a lovely time to die.

IRENE. And it will be again. Just try to think positive.

DEATH. I assure you I am doing my best.

IRENE. Good. Now, I say, let's get on with the business at hand while we have Mr. Pike's attention.

INSPECTOR. Mrs Hedges is absolutely right. Tell me, Mr. Pike, how's life?

PIKE. Couldn't be better.

INSPECTOR. No major disappointments?

PIKE. None.

JANE. You haven't awakened in the morning saying, "I wish I were dead"?

PIKE. Never.

INSPECTOR. Too bad.

PIKE. May I ask why?

IRENE. At first, Mr. Pike, this may sound a bit heartless and cruel, but it happens to be quite necessary, take my word for it. We are about to see if Death is able to do you in.

CONSTANCE. It's nothing personal, mind you.

DEATH. And I will try to make it as pleasant as possible.

MICHAEL. In any case, we hope you won't think the worst of it ... or us.

PIKE. Death! I'm here to be a victim of Death?

DEATH. Actually, just a subject. In this particular matter, I am the victim.

PIKE. How's that again? I'm to die and you're the victim?

IRENE. It's a long story, but in any case, we hope you don't mind.

PIKE. Of course not. Death, as it must, comes to all men. No one knows that better than I, or is it me?

INSPECTOR. For all practical purposes, let's just say it's you, and I do hope you have an enjoyable trip. (*To Death.*) He's all yours. Actually, I'm most curious to see how it's done.

DEATH. It's quite a simple thing, really. Fare-thee-well, Mr. Pike. (*HE waves his hand in front of Pike. Nothing happens.*) Die, Mr. Pike. Die, die, die.

JANE. Nothing's happening. How disappointing.

MICHAEL. Shhhhh!

DEATH. Fire, brimstone, lightning in sky. I am Death, and Death says die.

CONSTANCE. Nice bit of poetry, but it looks like that's all.

DEATH. Eye of Newt, Heart of Toad, Now 'tis time to hit the road.

INSPECTOR. Oh, come now. I think you're grasping at straws with that one.

DEATH. I can't do it. I can't do it anymore. Somehow I've lost my sting. Is it true? Am I ... Am I no longer ... Death?

IRENE. Frankly, I'm not so sure you ever were.

JANE. That makes two of us.

CONSTANCE. I can't tell you how disappointed I am that a fellow human being could pull such a cruel hoax on a nice bunch of innocent, warm, cordial people like us.

DEATH. (*Destroyed.*) But I am Death! I am!.... Or was.

IRENE. What a bunch of fools we must be to have believed all this rubbish, this supernatural, mystical nonsense.

JANE. To accept something so implausible. Especially someone as firmly grounded as I am.

MICHAEL. But what about Cousin Lester and Mr. Alfie Crown?

IRENE. A coincidence. A quirk of fate. Yes, it must have been strictly that and nothing more.

DEATH. No, no it wasn't. Everything about me, who I am, what I do, is true. You must not abandon me, Inspector. In the name of justice, decency and compassion, I beg you!

JANE. Oh, dry up.

IRENE. You know, Michael, we might just be able to make it to the Ridgley's this weekend after all. All we have to do is make arrangements for Cousin Lester's funeral.

MICHAEL. Maybe Mr. Pike could help us out there.

IRENE. Oh, yes. What a wonderful idea.

PIKE. My pleasure.

JANE. And what about Mr. Crown down there? I guess I could just dust around him for a few days.

IRENE. Why don't we just ask Mr. Pike to handle both of them. Mr. Crown and Cousin Lester. That's killing two birds with one stone, wouldn't you say?

DEATH. (*Sadly.*) I used to kill birds too.

PIKE. I'll be glad to handle everything, Mrs Hedges.

IRENE. Thank you. Actually this is all working out rather well. What uncanny luck, Mr. Pike being an undertaker.

JANE. Eerie is what I'd say.

CONSTANCE. Or maybe even morbid.

INSPECTOR. But so convenient.

PIKE. Needless to say, the pleasure is mine.

DEATH. And what about me? What becomes of me?

MICHAEL. Maybe we can take him with us to the Ridgley's for the weekend.

IRENE. I don't know, Michael. God knows that house is filled with enough curious pieces as it is.

DEATH. I feel so helpless, so lost. So all alone.

CONSTANCE. What sign are you? If you're Sagittarius, you have nothing to worry about.

DEATH. (*To Inspector.*) Where will I go? What is my future? And who is the new Death? And why?

INSPECTOR. I believe Mr. Pike can answer that.

MICHAEL. Mr. Pike?

CONSTANCE. How's that?

PIKE. I think you give me too much credit, Inspector.

INSPECTOR. And I think you give me too little, Mr. Jonathan Pike or whoever you really are.

(An evil smile crosses PIKE's face. HE begins to laugh. Slowly at first and then louder and louder. When HE stops there is a moment of silence as all look at him.)

MICHAEL. My God, what heavy dramatics. Does this mean we've stumbled onto still another poser?

JANE. Oh, I should hope not. My brain is already bursting with confusion and I haven't even talked to my old mother yet.

INSPECTOR. I'm still not sure what it all entails but I do know for a fact that Mr. Pike is not who he says he is. Especially an undertaker.

IRENE. Really? Oh, my. That means we're stuck with two bodies and it's almost dinner time.

INSPECTOR. You see, Mr. Pike, made one fatal error. In agreeing to lay the two deceased gentlemen to rest, Mr. Hedges and Mr. Crown, not once was the cost of interment mentioned. No legitimate undertaker I have ever known has such a generous nature.

PIKE. *(Smiling and applauding.)* Bravo, Inspector Mirabelle. Bravo!

CONSTANCE. My goodness, he looks so depressing and cadaverous, how could he be anything but an undertaker? And I mean that as a compliment, Mr. Pike.

INSPECTOR. It's the old story, "you can't tell a book by it's cover" even though that's where you usually find the title.

DEATH. Is it true, Mr. Pike? Are you not who you say you are?

PIKE. (*Looking out French doors.*) It's a beautiful day today. Would anyone be interested in a walk? It's very healthy.

INSPECTOR. I'm not so sure it will be with you. Who are you, Pike? Out with it!

(PIKE breaks out into a sinister laugh.)

MICHAEL. Careful, Inspector. I detect a menacing laugh.

PIKE. (*Indicating Death.*) Since you so readily seem to accept the fact that reprehensible demon of sleep over there, that sly, cunning, grim ferryman, that master of darkness and sorrow, is indeed Death, I really don't see why I should keep it from you any longer. Ladies and gentlemen, I am Life.

(Once again PIKE begins laughing sinisterly. DEATH looks at him for a beat and then rushes to him and begins strangling him with his bare hands. as ALL look on helplessly.)

INSPECTOR. A struggle between life and death. This is definitely my most interesting case.

(PIKE continues to laugh.)

CURTAIN

END OF ACT I

#2 intermission music

ACT II

Scene 1

Several hours later. Evening. The Hedges study. The room is dark. ALFIE's body lies where he has fallen, except now it is covered with a sheet. Suddenly a loud clap of THUNDER is heard and the room is illuminated by several flashes of LIGHTNING. When the room becomes quiet again, a SPOTLIGHT beams down on Alfie's covered body. ALFIE, still covered, sits up. The sheet falls to his waist as HE looks at the audience for a moment and smiles. There are more THUNDER and LIGHTNING flashes. When the room quiets down again, ALFIE stands in the SPOTLIGHT and sings and dances to "If I Had My Life To Live Over." After HE finishes the song HE sits where he originally fell, covers himself up with the sheet and lies back down, dead. The SPOTLIGHT goes off. There is another clap of THUNDER, a flash of LIGHTNING and the room goes dark. Instantly the LIGHTS switch on and MICHAEL and INSPECTOR MIRABELLE enter.*

---

* **Please note:**
Mention is made of songs which may or may not be in the public domain. Producers of this play are hereby CAUTIONED that permission to produce this play does not include rights to use these songs in production. Producers should contact the copyright owners directly for rights.

INSPECTOR. That was an excellent meal, excellent. From the vichyssoise to the leg of lamb, it was perfection. I can see why you and your wife were so concerned over losing your housekeeper.

MICHAEL. Yes, it's so rare you find a domestic nowadays who's an excellent cook as well as someone you can stand to live with. They are either gifted with one skill or the other.

INSPECTOR. I'm afraid we're living in an age of compromise. I submit, it all began when we outlawed capital punishment.

MICHAEL. (*At liquor cart.*) You may be right. Port?

INSPECTOR. Yes, that would be nice.

(MICHAEL pours two glasses of port and hands Mirabelle one.)

MICHAEL. Cheers.

INSPECTOR. Cheers.

BOTH. Well?

INSPECTOR. You first.

MICHAEL. I can't quite make it out.

INSPECTOR. Yes, it does seem a bit cloudy, doesn't it?

MICHAEL. We seem to be involved in some sort of esoteric hooliganism.

INSPECTOR. Don't we.

MICHAEL. Yet with monumental overtones.

INSPECTOR. I couldn't agree with you more.

MICHAEL. Think of it. Life and Death at the same dinner table. The significance is overwhelming.

INSPECTOR. Absolutely.

MICHAEL. Yet, to be honest, the meaning of it all, completely escapes me.

INSPECTOR. (*Nods.*) Pity, isn't it.

MICHAEL. What about you, Inspector? Have you made anything of it yet?

INSPECTOR. I have my theories but offering them at this early a juncture might only confuse us more.

MICHAEL. Yes. I can see that it might. You know, I don't really find him very likeable.

INSPECTOR. Who?

MICHAEL. Pike ... or Life ... or whatever he calls himself.

INSPECTOR. No, he doesn't seem to conduct himself in the manner one would expect from someone claiming to represent such a positive aspect of our existence.

MICHAEL. And that crass, hideous laugh of his. Really, it's most annoying. And all those terrible ethnic jokes. I have never been so embarrassed at the dinner table.

INSPECTOR. They certainly weren't called for, although the one about the Nun and the Penguin did extort more than a chuckle from me.

MICHAEL. Yes, well, in my estimation that was the only decent one.

(IRENE and CONSTANCE enter the room.)

INSPECTOR. Ladies.

IRENE. I dare say that was an adventure. I was speechless. The most obnoxious, classless chap I've had the displeasure of dining with in my entire life.

CONSTANCE. The way he talked and chewed his food at the same time. Even I was appalled.

IRENE. Never have I heard vichyssoise slurped so boldly. And the way he ate his salad with his dinner fork and his dinner with his salad fork. I absolutely shook inside with laughter.

MICHAEL. I don't think we were the only ones dismayed by his lack of social graces. During the main course I overheard Death whisper to him, in a less than tolerant voice, that his sleeve was not the proper cloth with which to wipe his mouth.

CONSTANCE. Oh, and what about the unfortunate incident with the gravy. Now was that an absolute debacle or not?

INSPECTOR. I fear the spilt gravy was my doing entirely. As I was passing the bowl to him, I noticed potato on his nose and I couldn't contain myself. The vessel just seemed to shake loose from my hand.

IRENE. A more than reasonable reaction, I must say. Fortunately most of the liquid was soaked up by the poor wretch's jacket so there wasn't much harm done.

CONSTANCE. He was lucky to be wearing that tweed suit, although it is a bit early in the season for that sort of heavy fabric, don't you think?

INSPECTOR. Yes. In most circles, tweed is actually frowned upon until after the first of October.

IRENE. One would hope so. But I did enjoy the presence of Death. His conversation sparkled with both wit and charm. He was the absolute epitome of aristocratic gentility.

INSPECTOR. Indeed. And his dining habits were impeccable, weren't they?

CONSTANCE. Oh, my, they were. Even I noticed that.

MICHAEL. Tell me, was I the only one who found it rather peculiar the way the two of them got on so well? Especially since earlier in the evening they would have killed each other had we not pulled them apart.

IRENE. As a matter of fact, I found it a bit peculiar myself.... I find it even more peculiar that at this very moment, they are strolling in the garden, chatting away like long lost friends. And you, Inspector? Do you find it peculiar also?

INSPECTOR. No. I prefer to use the word, curious. It's just as speculative a word, yet contains a bit more mystery, which in a peculiar sort of way is my game you know. But then again, I've always been intrigued by adjectives.

MICHAEL. Really? I'm sure it must go back to your childhood. Port, ladies?

IRENE. Yes. I think we should all love some.

(MICHAEL pours the ladies some wine.)

CONSTANCE. I have a confession to make. During that ill-behaved physical encounter, I actually found myself rooting for Death.

INSPECTOR. Really?

CONSTANCE. Of course. After all, he's so much more agreeable to look at. Do you find that shallow of me?

INSPECTOR. Not at all. It's the way America has been picking its leaders for years.

IRENE. Do you really think that Mr. Pike is Life? It's so surreal a concept.

INSPECTOR. You seem to accept Death.

IRENE. True, but it's so much easier to let credibility stretch when a gentleman is involved. Breeding does merit an edge.

INSPECTOR. So it seems, which once more indicates how unfair life really is.

(There is a clap of THUNDER and LIGHTNING flashes and then a quiet beat as DEATH and PIKE enter from the French doors.)

DEATH. You have a beautiful garden, Mrs. Hedges.

IRENE. Thank you. I take great pains with the esthetic ever since I read somewhere that one *is* what one chooses to see.

PIKE. Really? Maybe that's why I have such an affinity for mirrors. (*PIKE laughs raucously. THEY all look at him in disgust.*) I thought that was a real ripper.

MICHAEL. My wife takes great pride in her roses. Some have said they're the finest in all London.

DEATH. I adore roses. Unfortunately, for some reason, when I touch them they turn black.

CONSTANCE. How sad.

INSPECTOR. Yes. I imagine there are a number of things you have had to miss out on being who you are ... or were. But perhaps that will all change.

DEATH. Perhaps

INSPECTOR. Yes. Perhaps.

(PIKE has been inspecting several covered candy dishes. HE finds chocolates in one.)

PIKE. Oh, chocolates. (*HE grabs a handful and begins eating them.*) The second greatest invention in life.

INSPECTOR. Really? And the first?

PIKE. The hot plate of course. (*HE laughs at his joke. HE is the only one.*)

MICHAEL. The hot plate?

PIKE. It's an inside joke that for the time being I can only share with myself.

INSPECTOR. Before you two entered the room, we were commenting on how well you seem to be getting on.

DEATH. Yes, we are, aren't we? In the garden we had a fascinating discussion which I found quite enlightening.

IRENE. Really? About what?

DEATH. About the meaning of life. Actually, as strange as it seems coming from me, I have always felt life should be treated with the greatest dignity and respect, so that upon leaving it, one would feel a noble and pure fulfillment.

CONSTANCE. Oh, that's such a lofty thought. I'm impressed.

INSPECTOR. And Mr. Pike?

PIKE. Life! For God's sake why can't you call me Life! If you can call this knave, Death, you can surely call me, Life.

MICHAEL. A bit testy this evening, aren't we?

INSPECTOR. No, he's absolutely right. Forgive me. In this situation, protocol is a bit fuzzy. Now then, Life, what meaning do you give to your existence?

PIKE. I'm not so sure you'll like it.

CONSTANCE. Oh, please. I'm dying to find .... No, I don't think I'll say that.

PIKE. Fertilizer!

MICHAEL. How's that?

PIKE. Fertilizer! The meaning of life is fertilizer.

INSPECTOR. Fertilizer?

PIKE. Yes.

CONSTANCE. Shit!

PIKE. Exactly.

IRENE. How disgusting.

CONSTANCE. My saying shit or life being shit?

MICHAEL. I think we should concentrate on the latter which, I believe, is greatly responsible for the former.

IRENE. Fertilizer! My goodness, what a depressing concept.

PIKE. Oh, it is, I'm well aware of that, but those are the facts. Man is here solely to enrich the soil. That's why I think from the time one is born until the time one dies, one should have the best damn time ever and to hell with everything else.

IRENE. A totally pagan philosophy if ever I heard one.

PIKE. Of course. But even a so called civilized philosophy couldn't change man's destiny or function one iota.

CONSTANCE. I feel nauseas.

PIKE. Oh, come now. Why should it matter anyway? Once one is dead, one is dead. On earth, anyway, that is. (*HE pours himself a glass of wine.*)

IRENE. You mean there is something more after death?

CONSTANCE. Oh, wouldn't that be heaven?

PIKE. For some of us, possibly. (*PIKE breaks into a brief, wicked cackle and then lifts his wine glass in a toast.*) To me! (*HE drinks it down and wipes his mouth with his sleeve and laughs wickedly.*) I do have such a fine time with myself.

MICHAEL. My curiosity has been peaked. Is there really something after death?

PIKE. My goodness, how you would all like to know.

IRENE. I don't see what would be the harm. Just imagine how wonderful our lives would be if we knew what lay ahead ... if it were pleasant, of course. Never to fear death again. It would change the whole concept of human existence.

CONSTANCE. Not to mention ones attitude towards time. What you don't finish here, you can finish there. And once and for all we'd know if religion actually has any validity or if they've just been bluffing all this time.

INSPECTOR. Does anyone really think it would be a better world if there was no fear of the hereafter? From what I've seen in my line of work, I not only envision a horrendous outbreak in crime, but uncontrollable government spending as well.

DEATH. Do I note a touch of cynicism, Inspector?

INSPECTOR. When dealing with the real world, one must be a realist.

PIKE. I've always found reality such a muddy area. It has become so overcrowded with possibilities, lately only the lawyers seem to be able to get the best of it. (*HE laughs.*) Maybe, Inspector Mirabelle, the adventure of life is based on confusion.

INSPECTOR. For you, possibly. But for me, certainty reigns supreme.

(PIKE laughs again. Once more there is a clap of THUNDER and LIGHTNING flashes as the LIGHTS in the house flicker on and off.)

IRENE. God, but I hate that lightning and thunder ruckus. Does it have any dire significance or is it simply meant to scare the bloody pants off of us?

JANE. (*Enters.*) Excuse me, ma'am. I've got all the dishes put away and I've shampooed the carpet where Mr. Pike sat so that the food stains hardly show and I was wondering if you'd be needing my services anymore?

IRENE. No, I don't think so. I'm sure it's been a trying day for you too. Why don't you just take the rest of the evening off.

JANE. Why, thank you, Mrs. Hedges. That's most generous seeing it's not even near an important holiday. (*JANE crosses to the port, takes a big glass and, as all eyes watch her, fills it up with the wine.*) Frankly, the day going as it has, I've been giving some serious consideration to my serving notice.

IRENE. Oh, no.

JANE. Please, it's nothing personal, it's just that with so many weighty revelations brought on by this evening, I'm not so sure I can continue to be fulfilled by my lack of importance.

IRENE. Don't be silly, Jane. Of course you can. Everyone has insecurities from time to time.

JANE. Well, you all go on with what you're doing. I'll just sit here in Mr. Hedges favorite chair and continue to dwell on it a little more. But it's possible for my own self respect I may have to stop faking contentment for awhile. (*SHE holds up her filled glass in a toast.*) Cheers! (*SHE sits.*)

IRENE. Oh, my.

INSPECTOR. I, too, have been giving this situation a great deal of thought. Just what is the crime here? Life has replaced Death. I see no harm in that. And isn't that what Death wanted to know? To find out who has replaced him?

MICHAEL. Why, yes. That's what he did say.

IRENE. Oh, good. Then for all intents and purposes, we can consider the case closed and deem this chance encounter just one of those things.

CONSTANCE. That would be lovely. I really do need to get back to work.

IRENE. I'll tell you what. Let's all have a toast to the deceased Alfie Crown, there on the floor, as well as our poor, recently departed, cousin Lester, and then you can all toddle off to your respective homes, morgues or heaven knows where, humming the happy tune of your choice.

INSPECTOR. A lovely idea, Mrs. Hedges, but unfortunately, I, being who I am, have never been able to call a case closed until every aspect of my curiosity has been satisfied. You see it is not only necessary for me to find out *who*, it is my misfortune to need to find out *why*. Ladies and gentlemen, we are involved in a puzzle much trickier than it seemed at first, and I'm afraid there still are some missing pieces.

PIKE. Missing pieces of a puzzle? Really, Inspector. Somewhat cliche verbiage for one as gifted as you.

INSPECTOR. True, but in a convoluted matter such as this, I find simplicity a breath of fresh air. Now then, wouldn't it indeed be a calamity if the missing pieces weren't even in the puzzle box.

IRENE. My goodness. Now that would be something to ponder.

INSPECTOR. Or what if there were too many pieces to begin with? That would be another unfortunate turn of events.

MICHAEL. Yes. That's also a negative possibility.

INSPECTOR. And then again, it's possible that we're working with more than one puzzle.

CONSTANCE. Oh, my. What a quandary.

INSPECTOR. But let me give fair warning. My expert training has prepared me for any or all of the above.

JANE. Good for you, Copper.

IRENE. Jane!

JANE. I'm just trying to be encouraging, ma'am. Frankly I think he has a better chance of swimming to the moon than figuring this one out.

DEATH. Am I the only one who's aware that in the Inspector's long and illustrious career, he has never come out on the short end of it yet.

(The INSPECTOR and DEATH exchange looks.)

IRENE. Is that true, Inspector Mirabelle? Frankly, from your modus operandi, I would have guessed just the opposite. Of course, I recall, you did say that was the impression you felt comfortable conveying.

INSPECTOR. At the beginning, when some of the major clues are yet to be sniffed out, the answer is, yes. But as the case progresses, I find it extremely beneficial to let the culprit know who he is up against. I'm not sure if I do that solely to unhinge the doomed chap or merely out of professional courtesy. Therefore, let me serve notice now that it is indeed true, no case has ever proven my match. Yet, what perplexes me to a degree about this case is ...

DEATH. *(A beat.)* Yes?

INSPECTOR. Is this one really a case or ...

MICHAEL. *(A beat.)* Or what?

INSPECTOR. Or merely a game. Or ...

PIKE. (*A beat.*) Or what?

INSPECTOR. Or possibly both. In any event there has never failed to be a slip up or two and when that fatal miscalculation in judgement occurs, I shall pounce like a jackal upon a rabbit and end this beguiling, yet bewildering, conundrum to everyone's satisfaction.

JANE. (*Stands up and applauds.*) Finally I'm seeing my tax money at work. (*SHE gulps down her wine and begins pouring herself another.*) You know, I never have figured out why you silly rich end up with the houses, the money and the positions when it always seems to be the hired help that is constantly grounded in some sort of reasonable reality.

IRENE Please, Jane, let us not turn what seems to be a somewhat adventurous get together into another mundane class struggle.

INSPECTOR. Your mistress is absolutely right. We cannot afford to cloud the evening with issues. Therefore, it would please me greatly if everyone would continue with their small talk.

PIKE. My goodness. I doubt that there are many people who would consider a conversation with Life and Death as small talk.

INSPECTOR. True. But then again, are we really engaged in a conversation or merely shadow boxing with each other?

(DEATH sits at the piano and begins playing a beautiful waltz.)

CONSTANCE. Why that's beautiful.

DEATH. It's by Strauss, I believe. Wonderful musician, but a wretched man. Much too strict with the children.

CONSTANCE. As a child I had a music box that played that very tune. I came from extremely poor circumstances and it was the only nice thing I possessed. I remember how I would sit in my room and listen to my music box by the hour. I would imagine myself in a large, splendid ballroom dressed in a stunning, but tasteful, white gown, and while everyone was watching, I would be dancing with the handsomest prince in the world.

PIKE. A truly lovely story. By any chance were you wearing glass slippers? (*HE laughs at his joke. HE is the only one. Unmoved by the lack of response HE goes to the candy dish and helps himself to more of its contents which HE continues to eat during the following.*)

CONSTANCE. The music just makes you want to float on air, doesn't it?

(SHE begins dancing around the room. DEATH looks at her, rises and approaches her as the PIANO playing continues.)

DEATH. (*Offering to dance with her.*) May I?

CONSTANCE. Why yes. I'd be honored. (*The TWO dance.*)

DEATH. Excuse my boldness but did anyone ever tell you that your eyes are infatuating.

CONSTANCE. Why, no. No one ever seemed to look that high.

JANE. Isn't that a sight. It would give me the creeps if I saw this on the telly.

IRENE. What an utterly romantic pair they make.

MICHAEL. Yes, a dance with Death. One must be impressed by the spectacle if not the symbolism.

INSPECTOR. And I am impressed by the breakthrough that usually comes when I play my hand patiently.

DEATH. (*Stops dancing.*) A breakthrough?

IRENE. You've made a breakthrough so soon?

JANE. I knew the flatfoot would nail it down.

INSPECTOR. All it took was a simple, yet intelligent, observation. An observation so steeped in concrete credibility that it only enhances the less tangible suspicions I have had until now concerning the truths of this unearthly event which will shortly pour forth like an open floodgate from the valley of deception.

CONSTANCE. I seem to be missing something here, Inspector. Would you be so kind as to repeat what came after the maid said, "I knew the flatfoot would nail it down."

MICHAEL. Yes. What exactly is this breakthrough?

INSPECTOR. Think for a moment. If Death has indeed lost all his powers, as he says he has, how did he manage to keep the piano playing while he was off dancing? (*The INSPECTOR smiles triumphantly. There is a beat.*)

DEATH. Who would like to break the bad news to the Inspector? (*HE continues his dance with Constance.*)

INSPECTOR. (*Meekly.*) Bad news?

IRENE. Inspector, it's a player piano.

INSPECTOR. (*Disappointed.*) It is? (*HE inspects the piano.)*

MICHAEL. At an early juncture of our marriage, we had a choice of having children or buying a player piano.

IRENE. We have never regretted our decision.

INSPECTOR. So it is. A player piano. Oh, well. Live and learn I always say.

PIKE. My my. Another fumble for the Inspector. Could this be the beginning of the end of a legend?

DEATH. You said you had other suspicions, Inspector. Why not reveal them now?

MICHAEL. Perhaps you should. As a somewhat successful Bridge player, I can offer that there are occasions when one should not wait too long to play one's trump cards.

PIKE. Unless, of course, he's holding no trump cards.

INSPECTOR. It's been my rule of thumb that when one is holding no trump cards, he has a choice of passing, or biding one no-trump. Do you play the piano, Mr. Pike?

PIKE. Life, damn it! I'm Life! And no, I don't play the piano.

INSPECTOR. Too bad. It's a fabulous instrument, if mastered properly. (*The INSPECTOR sits down and plays a duet with the PIANO. HE is amazingly good.*)

IRENE. Why that's marvelous, Inspector. I never would have guessed that a man as basic as yourself would play anything but possibly a banjo.

INSPECTOR. Yes, most people are quite surprised, however, I do play the banjo as well, and probably would have enjoyed a wonderful career in music if only my inquisitive nature hadn't taken me elsewhere. Curiosity ... Curiosity ... What a curse for some of us to be blessed with. A rather dangerous blessing at times, yet one that might make this evening even more intriguing.

JANE. The bloody G-Man's on a roll.

DEATH. For the sake of your self esteem, Inspector, I do hope we've experienced the last of more faulty conjecture.

INSPECTOR. From the very beginning of this extravagant adventure, one word and one word only, seemed to play the major role. That word was "*why*." *Why* was all this happening? *Why* had Death lost his power? *Why* had Life been chosen to replace him. *Why* this particular arena, *why* us to witness it, and the biggest "why" of all ... If this ... (*Indicates Pike.*) ... chap here is really Life, *why* such an unbearable clod? (*The MUSIC ends. MIRABELLE emphasizes the following line by striking various piano keys to accent the word, "why."*) *Why, why, why, why, why* and another *why* for good measure. (*The INSPECTOR rises.*) The middle F key is off by one sixteenth of a tone.

(There is a beat.)

JANE. If I'm not mistaken, I believe the ball's in Life's court.

(Once more PIKE breaks into one of his evil laughs which is again followed by THUNDER, LIGHTNING flashes and the flickering of the LIGHTS.)

PIKE. From where I stand, there actually seems to be a good deal of all of you in me, possibly too much for anyone's discriminating conventionalities. What I am, is what I am. A clod ... if that's what you see. An ill mannered, vulgar, obnoxious oaf ... if that is what you see. What is life anyway? Wonderful? Rotten? Magnificent? Unfair? Joyous? Miserable? It's anything to anyone and everything to everyone. But now there are other implications. For Life to be in charge of Death. Think of it. Oh, I am not professing that people would no longer die. The planet would be in absolute chaos if that were to happen. What I mean to implement now is simply a happier, lighter approach to our ultimate fate. I mean to have us look forward to our expiration with the same joy that greeted our entry. Is that possible you ask? I, for one, think so for immediately upon birth I would let everyone know when that person's death would come. Then there would be two celebrations a year, a birthday and a deathday. Every year we'd have cake and candles and fun and laughter and then a day or so before that great and final fare-thee-well comes along, we'd make it a terrific event. Women in long dresses, men in white tie and tails, violins, flutes, cellos, or if you like, we go the rock and roll road. But we're all there with smiles, the widow to be, the orphans to be, the bereaved to be, all paying homage to that person about not to be. Now let's talk menu. Thumbs down on buffets. For these final moments let's make it a full course sit down dinner, soup, salad, entree and a dessert ... My God, the caterers of the world will love it. Hotel and restaurant space will be at a premium. A whole new economy will blossom forth. It might even replace war as the major source of expenditure and profit. We'll need a song, of course. Something bouncy and to the point like "So Long It's Been Good To Know You." Oh, yes, a funeral would be a much more pleasant thing to attend and the condolence cards would be a lot cheerier too. Possibly even humorous, like, "Sorry you're dead, but it's better than being sick." Maybe they'd put the obits next to the funnies. (*HE laughs wickedly again.*) Yes, sir, I'm definitely an idea whose time has come. What do you say? Let's hear it for me.

CONSTANCE. You're disgusting.

IRENE. I couldn't agree more. To make a mockery of Death. It's practically blasphemy.

JANE. Here! Here!

MICHAEL. How anyone can be so blasé over so sanctimonious an occasion as one's own end is beyond me. Taste, my good man, there is such a thing as taste. Really, next to you, Death is a Saint.

JANE. Here! Here!

IRENE. Oh, shut up, Jane. (*To Pike.*) To handle one's departure with little more than scornful contempt is absolutely intolerable, and I for one find it completely unacceptable.

CONSTANCE. I for one, find much more comfort in wailing and breastbeating or sack cloth and ashes.

MICHAEL. You're an unprincipled boor, Mr. Pike, or whoever you call yourself, and, frankly, the sooner you leave our presence, the better.

(The ROOM echoes agreement.)

INSPECTOR. My, my, what have we here? (*Pats Pike on the back sympathetically.*) An absolutely negative look at life. A feeling of repulsion, disenchantment, utter displeasure ...

JANE. I vote for all those things.

INSPECTOR. My dear friends, in an unusually clever way, we were all witness to the fact that Death lost his power. And what was our reaction?

CONSTANCE. I don't know about anyone else, but I felt sorry for the handsome gent.

DEATH. From our very first meeting, I thought you a woman of great compassion.

CONSTANCE. You flatter me, sir.

DEATH. Exactly my intent.

INSPECTOR. Sorry! Keep in mind that word. Sorry for Death who has come on numerous occasions to take away a lover, a father, a mother from her child, a child from his mother.... We have come to feel compassion, and empathy ... A strange feeling to have for an executioner isn't it?

MICHAEL. My goodness, yes. We have stopped thinking of Death in the negative, haven't we?

INSPECTOR. And as for Life, what have been our feelings for him? Contempt, disgust ... outrage.

PIKE. Anyone care to hear a few good racial jokes?

INSPECTOR. I offer this ... That we are mere dupes in the grand scheme of an all-powerful egotist. Life replacing Death. Ha! An imbecilic notion at best. For if there is one thing we can be sure of in life, it is that there is no escaping Death in any form that it appears. Death is death. Death has a job to do, and as such, mark my word, he will get it done. So we are back to the question of "why?". Why are we here and involved in this supernatural experience in a world where the supernatural only exists in movies, books, and on rare occasions, even plays? Ladies and gentlemen, what we have experienced was an attempt to allow something as despicable as Death to feel emotions he has never experienced before. Sympathy, warmth, human kindness and, if I hadn't caught on to it in time, possibly a love affair with Lady Constance.

CONSTANCE. Really? I'm not sure what my feelings are now. On one hand I'm terrified by the thought. On the other hand, one never knows who Mr. Right may be.

INSPECTOR. This whole escapade, this charade, is nothing but an amusement, an appalling entertainment for Mr. Death.

DEATH. Words, words, words.

INSPECTOR. Hamlet. Act Two. Scene Three.

PIKE. Act Two, Scene Two, you pompous ass.

INSPECTOR. Of course. Who then but an actor would know.

MICHAEL. An actor?

(During the following, ALFIE rises unnoticed and picks up a nearby piece of statuary to use as a weapon and starts towards the Inspector.)

INSPECTOR. I'm afraid I was suspect of Mr. Pike from the moment he arrived. As previously pointed out, it is indeed too early in the season for tweeds, giving credence to the theory that only those with one good suit might be forced into such an embarrassing predicament. Heavily steeped in theatrical lore as I am, I know that it is very rare you find an actor of the stage possessing more than one good suit. It just happens to be the economics of the theater. And as you all have just witnessed, his correcting me on my Shakespeare verifies his true profession. Secondly, my spilling gravy, earlier this evening, on Mr. Pike's jacket wasn't just an act of carelessness. Professing to be Life, it crossed my mind as to whether or not his jacket would have a label on it.

IRENE. What a brilliant notion.

INSPECTOR. Of course.

MICHAEL. And did it?

INSPECTOR. I found it quite difficult to believe that an omnipotent force such as Life would wear a suit from Marks and Spenser.

IRENE. Oh, no. They have marvelous buys on cashmere sweaters but I'm afraid their suits are not quite up to snuff.

(As ALFIE is about to bring his weapon down on the Inspector's head, JANE sees him and screams. The room is once again illuminated with LIGHTNING flashes and the sound of THUNDER. The INSPECTOR ducks out of the way in time causing ALFIE to lose his balance and topple over a chair. The INSPECTOR takes Alfie's weapon from him and helps him up.)

INSPECTOR. I'll take that.

CONSTANCE. Alfie! You're alive.

ALFIE. Why so I am! What a relief!

MICHAEL. My goodness, man. You were trying to kill the Inspector.

ALFIE. Is that true? But why? I'm a landlord, not a criminal.

INSPECTOR. Careful, my good man. You walk a thin line on that one. Besides, it wasn't your doing. Apparently I'm getting much to close to some touchy answers.

IRENE. I've got to know. How was it being dead, Mr. Crown?

ALFIE. Not bad. You never seem to worry about unpaid bills anymore. Anything new since I left town?

IRENE. The Inspector was getting into the nitty-gritty of all this. By the way, you haven't met Mr. Pike who started out as an undertaker and now ends up being merely an actor.

ALFIE. Really? My condolences on your severe loss of income.

INSPECTOR. There were other clues that led me to believe Mr. Pike was nothing more than a thespian. Who but a stage actor would list a hot plate as the greatest invention of our time? How well, those, who on their lonely and precarious attempt to climb the theatrical ladder, know of the nourishment and companionship furnished by a can of broth and something to warm it on.

MICHAEL. Yes. That makes sense.

INSPECTOR. Of course. Now then, next to sleuthing and music, my other great love is the theater. In the last twenty years I have never missed a play on the London stage no matter what the reviews. I put forth that our friend, Mr. Pike or Life, is none other than the excellent but unheralded character actor, Ernest Edmonton. (*HE yanks a toupee from Pike's head.*)

PIKE. Hey! Give me that!

IRENE. Oh, my. A rug!

CONSTANCE. I recognize that face. Why that's the midget I saw outside of Lester's house.

MICHAEL. (*To Pike.*) You can play a midget?

PIKE. I'm a professional actor sir. I can play anything. (*PIKE takes the toupee and puts it back on his head.*) And for every ones's information, the reason I'm wearing tweeds is because my summer suit just happens to be at the cleaners.

INSPECTOR. I had the pleasure of seeing Mr. Edmondton the other night in the somewhat mediocre farce, *Lights Over Bombay*. Mr. Edmondton played the part of Tambor, the legless half caste.

ALFIE. So playing a midget must have been child's play for him, although I don't see what purpose it served.

INSPECTOR. I suspect it was nothing more than a red herring. There seem to have been several along the way.

PIKE. I play fish, I play animals, I once played a clogged fuel tank for a gasoline commercial.

IRENE. I'm surprised you found *Lights Over Bombay* mediocre, Inspector. I rather liked it myself.

MICHAEL. So did I. I just wonder how they got that elephant on so tiny a stage.

JANE. I never go to the theater anymore. It's too damn predictable, but I do like elephants.

IRENE. Did you see Cats? I loved Cats!

CONSTANCE. Do you know what I really loved? I loved Phantom. I mean, any man in a mask, that's my cup of tea.

MICHAEL. I'd just like to know how they made that damn chandelier fall down.

INSPECTOR. Please! The case, the case! We are drifting!

IRENE. Inspector, if Mr. Edmonton is indeed an actor, isn't he missing tonight's performance?

PIKE. Oh, no. The play closed last night. I was very lucky to be able to step into another role so quickly.

DEATH. And it was a wonderful final performance.

ALFIE. Oh, oh. Trouble.

PIKE. Final ... No! You promised if I went along with this, you'd let me live.

DEATH. And so you have. An extra twenty hours. A lifetime to a Mayfly.

PIKE. (*Backing away.*) No. You can't. I'm not ready. There's so many other parts I want to do. Falstaff, Fagin, Ophelia ... I do women great.

(DEATH snaps his finger. There is more LIGHTNING and THUNDER. PIKE dies.)

IRENE. So it's you who's creating all that clamor.

JANE. And ... (*Pointing at Pike and screaming.*) ... Murder!

DEATH. Not murder in the least. You see I was supposed to take Mr. Edmondton last night. It was to be an unfortunate but intriguing mishap. After the cast's final curtain call, the elephant was to accidentally sit on him.

IRENE. How sad that it didn't go that way. I'm sure the publicity would have kept the play running another two months.

CONSTANCE. Then you are truly Death and you haven't lost your power. And you've been toying with us ... with our feelings ... with our hearts.

JANE. He didn't toy with good old Pike's heart. I'd say he stopped it forever.

DEATH. (*Looking at Constance for a beat and then turning to the Inspector.*) I knew you were good, Inspector, but I had no idea how good.

INSPECTOR. Thank you. As you probably suspect by now, my faux pas about the player piano was merely a ploy to examine your face as you watched me bobble a bit. The glee it expressed convinced me how important it was to you that I fail.

MICHAEL. You mean you knew it was a player piano?

INSPECTOR. There is very little that escapes me, as you will discover when I finally do retire from the yard and begin supplementing my meager pension by adapting several of my rather spirited adventures into hair raising thrillers.

DEATH. Please, everyone. I beg you not to be too harsh with me. Yes, I wanted to feel something else besides fear and dread. I wanted to feel love and kindness and tenderness. And for a moment I did. And it was wonderful. And I thank you for it. If only you mortals wouldn't fear me so, my existence could be almost pleasant. You can't imagine what it's like to be hated, loathed, dreaded ... shunned ... reviled ...

IRENE. Oh, the poor man.

DEATH. Yes.

CONSTANCE. The dear soul.

DEATH. Yes.

MICHAEL. The sad wretch.

DEATH. Yes.

ALFIE. The unlucky bloke.

DEATH. Yes, yes, yes, yes, yes!

INSPECTOR. Look, he's doing it again. There you go feeling sorry for Death again.

DEATH. (*To Inspector.*) You know, you're a bit of a spoil sport aren't you?

MICHAEL. My, God, Mirabelle, even if you are right, and it seems you are, the significance of today's events is mind boggling. The importance of love, even to Death.

CONSTANCE. So much love is wasted on those who don't deserve or appreciate it. It seems so unfair that someone like Death, who needs it so desperately, must go without. I shall always admire his noble quest.

DEATH. Thank you. Your concern will not go unremembered. I would have wagered anything that no one could have unraveled this situation. Even the great Sherlock Holmes stumbled and fell against me. I'm impressed, Inspector. Truly impressed.

INSPECTOR. Of course. But there is one thing that still puzzles me. That fact that knowing of my infallible record, you still chose to let me go on.

DEATH. I hadn't planned to. But somehow it did seem to turn into more of a game, especially towards the "*dénouement*" when it looked like you might have me, and then not ... I must say I did experience a certain satisfaction ... or as you humans put it, a rush. It's too bad that there will be no prize awarded for your extravagant fete.

INSPECTOR. You mean to take us then?

DEATH. I will be gentle. I promise.

ALFIE. My goodness, there's going to be some run on sympathy cards when he leaves the neighborhood.

JANE. (*Screaming.*) Murder!

DEATH. And she's first!

INSPECTOR. It isn't fair. You played a game and you lost. Certainly there should be some consequences.

DEATH. As well you know, Death is not always fair.

INSPECTOR. You mean you don't mind going out a loser? Pity. Somehow I expected more from you, especially since we are in England where there still remains a touch of honor and good sportsmanship among men.

DEATH. Are you taunting me? If there's one thing I don't like it's to be taunted.

INSPECTOR. A lot of people taunt death, a lot of people defy death, a lot of people laugh in the face of death but just how many people beat death? Admit it, damn it. That's what I did. I beat Death. Admit it!

DEATH. I don't have to listen to this. Besides, outside of you, who will know or care?

INSPECTOR. You will. Long after we're gone you will know it and it will fester inside you until it consumes your every thought. Night after night. Year after year. Eon after eon. Beaten, beaten, beaten and by a mere mortal.

JANE. Keep after him, Inspector. I think you have him on the ropes.

DEATH. All right! All right! It's true, I am not too keen on today's outcome. But I have a proposition.

IRENE. A Proposition with Death. My goodness, I just felt a chill. Hopefully from the language.

DEATH. What say we try it again. One more case, one more game, but I assure you this one won't be as easy.

INSPECTOR. And the stakes?

DEATH. The same. Your life.

INSPECTOR. And if I win again?

DEATH. You won't, but should that doubtful result occur once more I give my word that you will never hear from me again until your natural time to depart.

INSPECTOR. And these others?

DEATH. You can't expect me to leave empty handed?

INSPECTOR. You already have an actor.

DEATH. True, but he isn't much of a trophy. At the dinner table those were his actual manners.

MICHAEL. It seems so wrong that one's existence should all come down to a game.

INSPECTOR. Maybe the message here is that Life is the game of avoiding death.

DEATH. Do we have a deal?

INSPECTOR. Yes. Providing you also agree to not willingly take anymore here tonight.

DEATH. Well, if I must. Okay. Done. So then, Inspector, to our next encounter, which I'm sure will have a more satisfactory conclusion for me.

INSPECTOR. Possibly. But then one never knows what life has in store for him.

DEATH. Yes. Unfortunately, that does seem to be the rule of thumb around here. I thank you all for your company and what brief amusement I sustained from your hospitality and concern.

CONSTANCE. And love? Did you feel any love?

DEATH. I ... I don't know.

CONSTANCE. It gives rather a feeling of butterflies in one's stomach.

DEATH. I'm sorry but I feel no abdominal insects at all. In fact, except for severe disappointment in this evenings outcome, I never felt better. Farewell, Inspector Mirabelle. You have won this one but it's proven gospel that no one beats Death forever.

INSPECTOR. Not forever. Not for long. But for the time being is good enough.

CONSTANCE. (*Running to Death.*) No! Wait! (*SHE embraces him for a kiss.*)

DEATH. Don't.

CONSTANCE. You must feel something more of life.

INSPECTOR. Stop, Miss Lawson.

(CONSTANCE kisses Death.)

INSPECTOR. My God! A kiss of death.

IRENE. Oh, my. I just felt another chill.

DEATH. (*To Constance. Shaken.*) I'm sorry. Very sorry.

CONSTANCE. Then it was worth it. (*SHE falls limp into Death's arms.*)

DEATH. (*To Mirabelle.*) This was not my will.

INSPECTOR. I know. It's not an easy world.

DEATH. Till we meet again, Mirabelle.

INSPECTOR. I look forward to it.

(The stage goes DARK. There is a flash of LIGHTNING and a clap of THUNDER. Again the LIGHTS flicker. DEATH disappears. JANE screams. The LIGHTS go on. The INSPECTOR, MICHAEL, IRENE, JANE and ALFIE now stand in the room. ALL seem confused. CONSTANCE lies dead on the sofa near the body of Pike.)

MICHAEL. What happened?

IRENE. Who are all these people?

JANE. I don't know. I was just dusting and there they were. *(JANE points to the bodies of Constance and Pike.)* Murder!

(THEY all go over to inspect the bodies.)

MICHAEL. Oh, my goodness. Dead bodies in my house. How did this happen?

ALFIE. Beats me. The last I remember I was trimming some bushes on my front lawn.

IRENE. Call the police! Someone call the police!

INSPECTOR. Madam, I am the police. Inspector Edward Mirabelle of the Yard, and my being here is also very strange. Very strange indeed.

MICHAEL. I don't understand. I really don't understand.

INSPECTOR. Neither do I yet, but I have a feeling this will be my most interesting case.

(ALL eyes are on the INSPECTOR, who slowly breaks into a smile.)

CURTAIN

THE END

curtain call music

COSTUME PLOT

DEATH
Black hooded cloak/robe

MICHAEL HEDGES
Lightweight conservative button-down cardigan sweater, shirt, tie, dark slacks

JANE
Maid's dress with small white apron

IRENE HEDGES
Conservative blouse and skirt

INSPECTOR MIRABELLE
Grey summer suit, white shirt, tie. He should have that worn detective look.

CONSTANCE LAWSON
Low-cut flamboyant dress, reds, purples, etc., hat and shoes, handbag

ALFIE CROWN
Sleeveless v-neck sweater, shirt, tie, light colored pants. The sleeves on his shirt are rolled up past his elbow.

JONATHAN PIKE
Loud woolen tweed suit, bold stripped shirt, dark tie

PROPERTY PLOT

Basic Set

Sofa
Two wing back chairs
Spinet piano
Liquor cart with glasses
Several small tables
Several bottles of port, brandy, sherry
Bookcases (can be in set walls)

Pre-Set Props

Act I

Copy of *London Times*
Cigarette box with cigarettes
Cigarette lighter
Ashtray
Telephone
Several candy dishes, one filled with chocolates
A small piece of statuary that can be held by hand and used as a weapon.

Other accessories as needed to give set an elegant, English feeling.

Act II

Bed sheet

Carry-On Props

I, 1
Feather duster (Jane)
Paper invitation, envelope (Irene)

I, 2
Calling card (Pike)

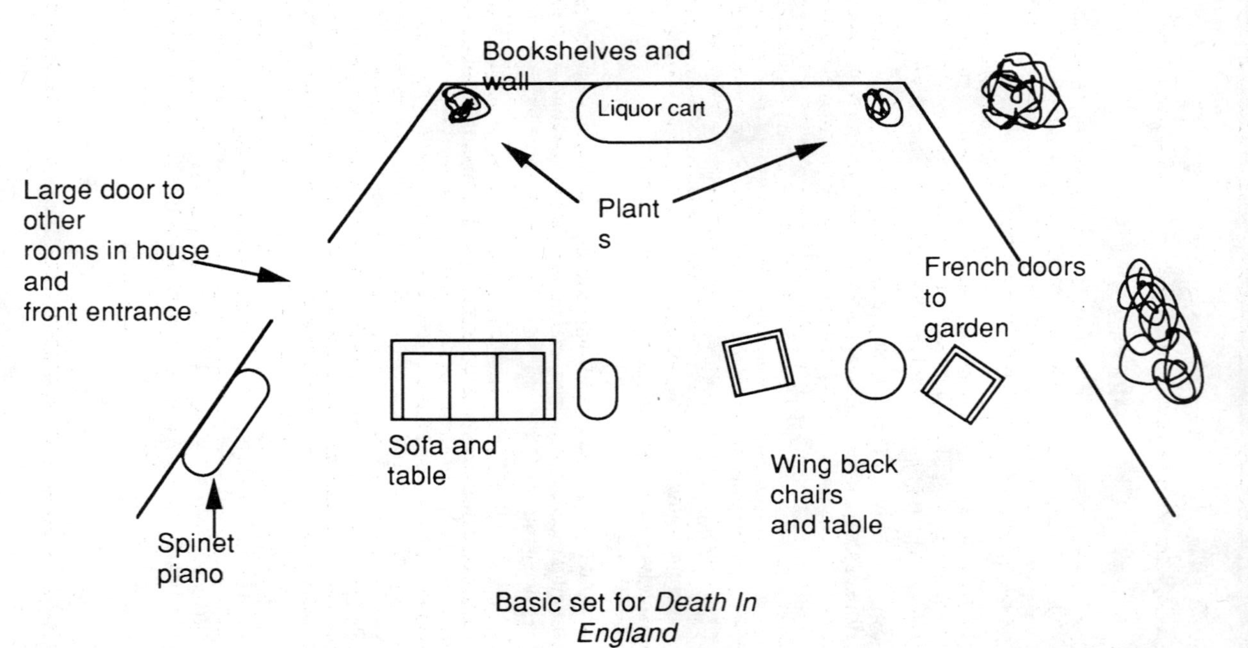

Basic set for *Death In England*

Other Publications For Your Interest

DOCTOR DEATH. (All Groups.) Thriller-Farce. Mark Chandler. 3m., 9f. (can also be 4m, 8f. or 5m., 7f., via two male or female roles) That pixilated playwright of merry murder is at it again: The author of the marvelous *I Shot My Rich Aunt* takes us this time to the French Riviera, on a pleasure yacht just off Cap d'Antibes, where the happy guests of a mysterious host discover they're all marked for a madman's murderous vengeance. Their first clue that this will be less than a pleasant outing arrives in a deck of Old Maid cards, in which each is named—and rather nastily described. And with this clue comes the horrifying realization that one of them is a cruel and calculating killer. But which one? Can the malevolent mastermind be lovely Linda Luscious, handsome Victor Valor, bartender Margarita Martini, steward Queenie Quill, TV hostess Wendy Windy, shy secretary Portia Peck, sleazy Ritchy Raunchy, private-eye Harry Hulk, math-expert Sibyl Service, wrestler Minnie Mountain, actress Fanny Flop, or aerobics advocate Jillian Jogger? They'd better find out soon, because just after they realize that none of them can swim a stroke, they learn that the yacht is slowly sinking! (And in shark-filled waters, to boot!) Can they unmask the fiend in their midst? Can they figure out how to get off the doomed ship without drowning—or worse—in the process? Thrill follows chill in this madcap melodrama of hideous revenge—and there are so many gut-busting laughs along the way that you'll lose count! We promise you, this is a highly unusual variation on the trapped-by-a killer genre. The setting, the characters, and the convoluted plot are all superbly fascinating—and absolutely hilarious. A wonderfully zany evening of fun! **#674**

I SHOT MY RICH AUNT. (All Groups.) Comedy. Mark Chandler. 4m., 5f. This rollicking romp through the British aristocracy's environs is a melange of off-the-wall farce and near-murder mystery. Every role is a gem and a delight for the performers. Lady Valonia Wendrew is having a number of people come to weekend at her stately manor (a former castle with a weird history) on the occasion of her nephew Dustin's announcement of his engagement to Judy Blake. Unluckily, Dustin's former flame Vivian Rexford has arrived to find out why Dustin dumped her two months previously, and Judy's brother Bingo Blake lets Dustin talk him into going outside to shoot at some starlings, and Lord Henry Mayhew, the family solicitor, is coming to change Valonia's will *out* of Dustin's favor, and Judy's school chum Gwendolyn Natterly is coming to meet—and ensnare—Dustin's cousin Nigel, a humble curate who thinks he's only there to meet Dustin's fiancee, and during the starling-shoot a stray bullet enters the library, and Dustin enters to find Valonia with a small hole in her blouse surrounded by oozing warm red liquid, and by the time he's run and gotten Bingo to come in and help him know what to do, the aunt's body has vanished and Eloise the maid is suspected to Know All and is planning to blackmail Dustin and meantime the picketing cooks' and maidservants' unions have raised the estate's drawbridge, thus entrapping everyone as night falls, and then Henry's wife thinks he's having an affair with Gwendolyn and she arrives with horsewhip in hand on the incoming fire engine (did we tell you the place is on fire?) You're going to be sore from the endless belly-laughs, all the way to the utterly insane finale! **#11103**

New Thrillers from Samuel French, Inc.

ACCOMPLICE. (Little Theatre). Thriller. Rupert Holmes. 2m., 2f., plus one surprise guest star. Int. This truly unique new thriller by the author *The Mystery of Edwin Drood* broke all box office records at the Pasadena Playhouse, and went on to thrill audiences on Broadway. Sorry, but the only way we can describe the amazing plot for you is to "give it away." *Accomplice* starts out as a straightforward English thriller, set in a country house, in which a sex-starved wife plans, with the help of her lover, to murder her stuffy husband. All is, of course, not as it first seems. Oh, yes!—the "husband" is murdered onstage; but, later, he re-enters! Why? Because what we have actually been watching is a dress rehearsal. The play takes a new twist when we learn that this is an out-of-town tryout. The "husband" we have just seen "murdered" is actually the playwright and director of the play-within-the-play, and *he* has plotted to murder his *wife*, the actress playing the lead in his play, so that he can proceed unimpeded with his affair with her leading man. Got that so far? Well—you ain't seen *nothing* yet! A surprise character comes out of the audience (no—we won't tell you who it is), revealing that, in actuality, something entirely different is going on. A cast member is being set up—brilliantly and effectively, it turns out; and the cast has its final revenge against a fellow thespian whose cruelty resulted in the suicide of a friend. "The show is a delight. It is humorous, odd, scary, wildly dramatic, adult, adolescent—in short, impossible to dislike."—Pasadena Star-News. "Miss it at your peril."—L.A. Herald Examiner. "Wonderfully entertaining . . . a breathless ride through an ever-shifting series of planes."—Cleveland Plain Dealer. "A total delight."—Bergen News. "Part murder mystery, part sex farce and completely entertaining . . . suspenseful, charming and funny."—USA Today. Slightly restricted. **(#3144)**

MAKING A KILLING. (Little Theatre.) Thriller. John Nassivera. 2m., 2f. Comb. Int. A Broadway playwright, his conniving producer and his actress wife hatch a plot to guarantee their new play will be a success; they fake the suicide of the playwright on opening night! They then high-tail it up to Vermont where the playwright hopes to disappear, as he hates the public spotlight anyway. However, after a few weeks the playwright decides he no longer wants to participate in the scheme. Maybe his wife and his producer (who are having an affair) will have to kill him for real! Also on the scene is the playwright's feisty agent, who uncovers the plot and then helps her client deal with his most difficult artistic challenge: foiling his producer and wife! "A magnificent mystery thriller ... wonderful entertainment."—Bennington Banner. "Absorbing theatre."—Schenectady Gazette. **(#15200)**

Other Publications For Your Interest

PICTURE OF DORIAN GRAY, THE. (Little Theatre.) Drama. Adapted by John Osborne from the novel by Oscar Wilde. 11m., 4f., plus extras. I Int. w/apron for other scenes. English playwright John Osborne (Look Back in Anger, Inadmissible Evidence, The Entertainer) has given us a brilliant dramatisation of Wilde's classic novel about a young man who, magically, retains his youth and beauty while the decay of advancing years and moral corruption only appears on a portrait painted by one of his lovers. Following the advice of the evil Lord Harry, a cynic who, fashionably, mocks any and all institutions and moral precepts, Dorian comes to believe that the only purpose of life is simply for one to realize, and glorify, one's own nature. In so doing, he is inevitably sucked into the maelstrom of degradation and despair, human nature being what it is. "Osborne has done much more than a scissors-and-paste job on Wilde's famous story. He has thinned out the over-abundant epigrams, he has highlighted the topical concept of youth as a commodity for which one would sell one's soul and he has, in Turn of the Screw fashion, created a sense of evil through implication. Osborne conveys moral disintegration through the gradual breakdown of the hero's language into terse, broken phrases and through a creeping phantasmagoria."—London, The Guardian. "What is so interesting about John Osborne's adaptation of The Picture of Dorian Gray is that he had found in Oscar Wilde's macabre morality a velveted barouche for his own favorite themes. Osborne funks none of the greenery-valley vulgarity of the fabulous story, and conveys much of its fascination."—London, Daily Telegraph. State author when ordering. **(#18954)**

FALL OF THE HOUSE OF USHER, THE. (Little Theatre.) Drama. Gip Hoppe. Music by Jay Hagenbuckle. 6m. 3f. Int. A comfortable suburban family man receives a desperate telephone call from an obscure and forgotten childhood acquaintance. Thus starts a journey into madness that will take Ed Allen to the House of Usher and the terrible secrets and temptations contained there. In this modern adaptation of the classic short story by Edgar Allen Poe, playwright Gip Hoppe takes Gothic horror into the 90s, questioning the definition of "sanity" in the same way Poe did in his day. Ed arrives to find Roderick in a state of panic and anxiety over the impending death of his sister, Madeline. As he tries to sort out the facts, he becomes tangled in a family web of incest and murder. Finding himself infatuated with the beautiful Madeline, his "outside life" fades from his memory as he descends to the depths of madness that inflict all the residents of The House of Usher. *The Fall of the House of Usher* is an exhilarating theatrical adventure leading to an apocalyptic ending that will have audiences thrilled. Actors and designers will be challenged in new ways in this unpredictable and wildly entertaining play. Cassette tape. Use of Mr. Hagenbuckle's music will greatly enhance the play, but it is not mandatory. **(#7991)**

FAVORITE MELODRAMAS

VIRTUE ALWAYS TRIUMPHS; or LIFE IN THE WICKED CITY. (Little Theatre.) Melodrama. Walter Boughton. 14m., 5f. (doubling possible). 3 ints. A damsel in distress named Charity takes refuge in Amos Truhart's house during a raging blizzard. She is trying to escape the clutches of the perfidious Warrington Chadbourne, after her because she is the sole heir to a huge railroad fortune. Chadbourne wants to marry her and then do her in for the money. While staying with the Truharts, Charity falls in love with their son, Tyrone, who forthwith proposes that they tie the nuptial knot; but Charity has a sordid past (so she thinks), so she declines. Our hero, Tyrone Truhart, is indefatigable in his devotion to Charity, even when Chadbourne frames Charity on a charge of having borne an illegitimate child. Charity leaves with the child and winds up on the Bowery, pursued hotly by Tyrone, who wants to rescue her and clear her name, and Chadbourne, who only cares about her money. Chadbourne finds her first, and threatens to kill the child unless she marries him. Will Tyrone come to the rescue in time? *Is* Charity the daughter of Slick Annie, the Fence, or someone else entirely? Well, to find out you'll just have to order a copy of this delightful, fast-paced new old-time "mellerdrammer." **(#24617)**

SAY UNCLE, UNCLE SILAS. (Trapped in a House of Fiends) (All Groups.) Melodrama Spoof. Tim Kelly. 9f., 5m. Simple Staging. Savage murders! Blackmail! Thunderstorms! Chewed scenery! And yes—romance! This is an hilarious laff-a-minute spoof of English Gothic melodramas. Suggested by Sheridan LeFanu's *Uncle Silas*. The setting is Barnum-Hogg, a grim edifice that looks like Wuthering Heights after a fire. Ghosts walk and tombstones in the graveyard "stick up like swollen thumbs." Enter Maud Ruthyn, a young heiress who'll remind you of Jane Eyre on a bad day. She soon finds herself menaced by her creepy relative who makes Sweeney Todd seem like a nice guy. To tutor our heroine he hires a monstrous governess, Madame De La Rougepot. Silas hopes to force Maud to marry his brute of a son, Dudley. However, Dudley has a secret wife! Silas formulates another plan to get Maud's fortune. It's a very nasty (and uproarious) scheme involving deception, deceit and more murder. Horrors! Will handsome Captain Oakley and sophisticated Lady Monica save Maud in time? Will the mystery of the locked room be revealed? Said one reviewer, "Subtle it's not, funny it is." Bad acting and cheap scenery can only help. Wonderfully goofy roles and no production hassles. An audience and cast pleaser. By the author of *Egad, The Woman in White* and *The Face on the Barroom Floor*. **(#20995)**